A Visit to CANADA

by William Anthony

Minneapolis, Minnesota

Credits

All images are courtesy of Shutterstock.com, unless otherwise specified. With thanks to Getty Images, Thinkstock Photo, and iStockphoto.

Cover – Bosnian, kavram. 2 – Weekend Warrior Photos. 4-5 – EB Adventure Photography, Alex Staroseltsev. 6-7 – Media Home, i viewfinder. 8-9 – Diego Grandi, Spiroview Inc. 10-11 – esfera, R.M. Nunes. 12-13 – FILMME, showcake, Werner Muenzker. 14-15 – ranmaru, CPQ. 16-17 – Bing Wen. 18-19 – Steve Gilbert, Robert Nyholm. 20-21 – Anne Kiel, Luna Vandoorne. 22-23 – Colin Temple, Ken Phung.

Library of Congress Cataloging-in-Publication Data is available at www.loc.gov or upon request from the publisher.

ISBN: 979-8-88509-370-5 (hardcover)
ISBN: 979-8-88509-492-4 (paperback)
ISBN: 979-8-88509-607-2 (ebook)

© 2023 Booklife Publishing
This edition is published by arrangement with Booklife Publishing.

North American adaptations © 2023 Bearport Publishing Company. All rights reserved. No part of this publication may be reproduced in whole or in part, stored in any retrieval system, or transmitted in any form or by any means, electronic, mechanical, photocopying, recording, or otherwise, without written permission from the publisher.

For more information, write to Bearport Publishing, 5357 Penn Avenue South, Minneapolis, MN 55419.

CONTENTS

Country to Country 4
Today's Trip Is to Canada! 6
Toronto 8
Canada and France 10
Food 12
Niagara Falls 14
Manito Ahbee Festival 16
Hockey 18
Animals 20
Before You Go 22
Glossary 24
Index 24

COUNTRY TO COUNTRY

A country is an area of land marked by **borders**. The people in each country have their own rules and ways of living. They may speak different languages.

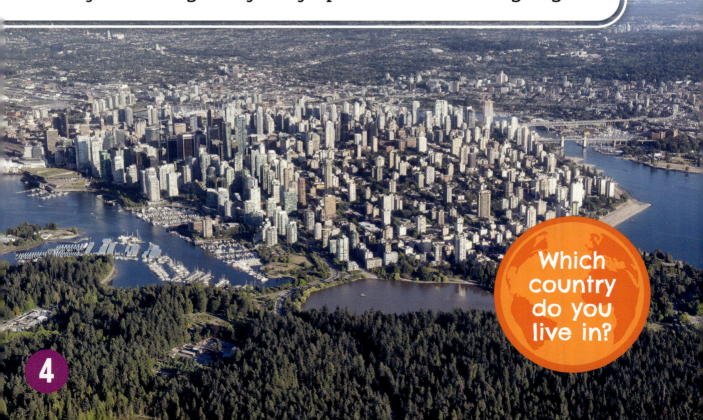

Which country do you live in?

Each country around the world has its own interesting things to see and do. Let's take a trip to visit a country and learn more!

Have you ever visited another country?

TODAY'S TRIP IS TO CANADA!

Canada is a country in the **continent** of North America.

FACT FILE

Capital city: Ottawa
Main languages: English and French
Currency: Canadian dollar
Flag:

Currency is the type of money that is used in a country.

TORONTO

We'll start our trip in Toronto! This city is in the **province** of Ontario. It has the largest **population** of any city in Canada.

CN Tower

At one time, the CN Tower was the tallest building in the world.

Toronto has lots of tall buildings. The tallest is the CN Tower. This structure stands 1,815 feet (553 m) tall and took more than 3 years to build.

CANADA AND FRANCE

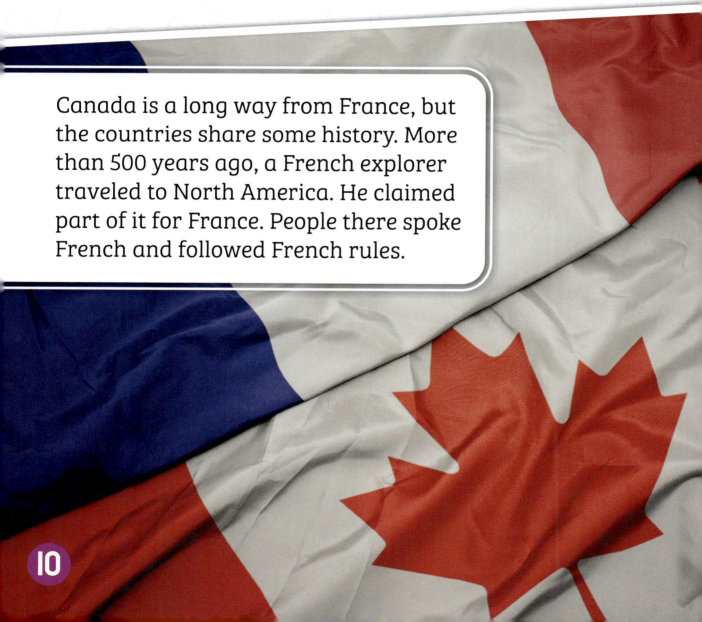

Canada is a long way from France, but the countries share some history. More than 500 years ago, a French explorer traveled to North America. He claimed part of it for France. People there spoke French and followed French rules.

Today, Canada is no longer **ruled** by France. But French is still one of Canada's main languages. In the province of Quebec, many people speak French as their first language.

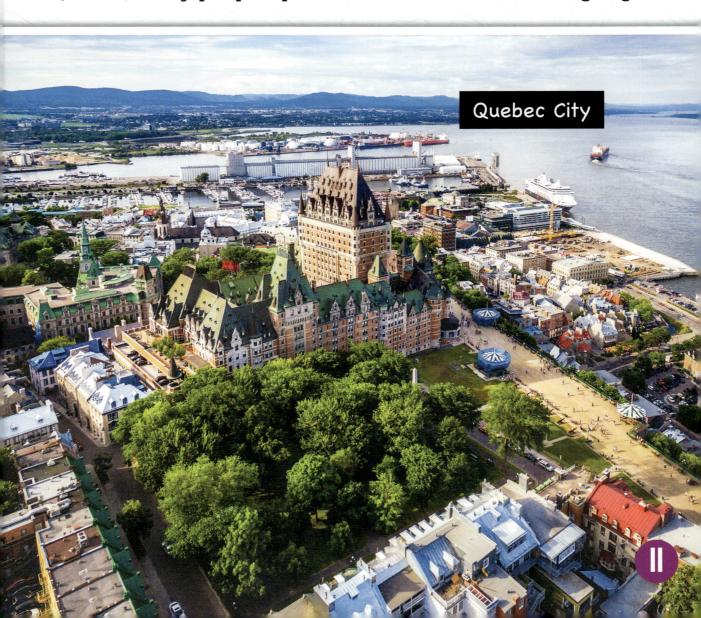

Quebec City

FOOD

Feeling hungry? Let's try some poutine! This yummy dish is made of French fries topped with gravy and chunks of cheese.

We could also try some maple syrup. Canada is famous for this sweet treat that comes from maple trees. There is even a maple leaf on Canada's flag!

NIAGARA FALLS

Next, let's head into nature to see one of Canada's most amazing sights. Niagara Falls is a group of three waterfalls on the border between Canada and the United States.

The waterfalls are named the American Falls, the Bridal Veil Falls, and the Horseshoe Falls. They are more than 12,000 years old.

The Horseshoe Falls are also called the Canadian Falls.

MANITO AHBEE FESTIVAL

Time to celebrate! The Manito Ahbee Festival celebrates the first groups of people to live in Canada. These groups are called First Nations.

The Manito Ahbee Festival happens every year in the city of Winnipeg. There is dancing and music. The festival teaches people about the **traditions** of First Nations.

HOCKEY

Let's play hockey! This is Canada's **national** winter sport.

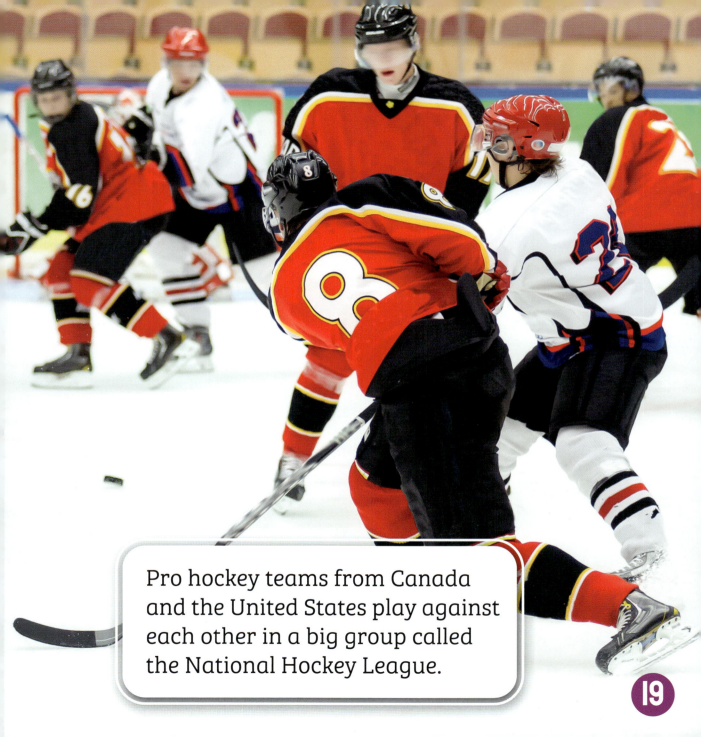

Pro hockey teams from Canada and the United States play against each other in a big group called the National Hockey League.

ANIMALS

Look at that mother with her cubs! Canada is home to some animals that are hard to find in other places. In northern parts of the country, you might spot polar bears.

Beluga whales swim through the ocean waters around Canada. Many people take boat trips to look for these animals.

BEFORE YOU GO

We can't forget to visit Rideau **Canal** in the city of Ottawa. During winter, the canal freezes and becomes a huge ice-skating rink!

We should also try to see the northern lights. These glowing colors appear in the sky during different times of the year. Canada is one of the best places to see them!

What have you learned about Canada on this trip?

GLOSSARY

borders lines on a map that show where one place ends and another begins

canal a small waterway built for boat travel or to move water

continent one of the world's seven large land masses

national something relating to an entire country

population the number of people that live in a place

province any one of the large parts that Canada is separated into

ruled to be controlled or under the power of a country's government or leader

traditions things that a group of people have done for many years

INDEX

CN Tower 9
First Nations 16–17
hockey 18–19
maple syrup 13
Niagara Falls 14–15
northern lights 23
polar bears 20
poutine 12
winter 18, 22